CONFESSIONS

Poetry Anthology

Volume III

CONFESSIONS

Poetry Anthology Volume III

Rian N. Jenkins

Copyright © 2024 by Rian N. Jenkins

All rights reserved, including the right of reproduction in whole or in part in any form. No part of this book may be reproduced, stored in, or introduced into a retrieval system, or transmitted, in any form or by any means (electronic, mechanical, photocopying, recording, or otherwise) without prior written permission from the author.

If you purchased this book without a cover, you should be aware that this book is stolen property. It was reported as "unsold and destroyed" to the publisher, and neither the author nor the publisher has received payment for this "stripped book."

ISBN: 978-1-7353316-1-4

Photography by Blu Graphics (Louis Jones)
Cover Designed by Rian N. Jenkins
Edited by Sharon Morgan
Published by Rian N. Jenkins
Crowned By Nichele, LLC
For information on the content of this book, email
crownedbynichele@gmail.com
www.riannjenkins.com

Printed in the United States of America

OTHER PROJECTS

A Queen's Heart, Poetry Anthology Volume I

A Queen's Anthem, Poetry Anthology Volume II

FUTURE PROJECTS

Confessions, Part Two, Poetry Anthology Volume IV

The Reverse Novel Series

LUKE BROWN

*This book is dedicated to all
who want to be heard and
need the courage to speak.*

Acknowledgments

In the process of putting this poetry anthology together, I didn't realize that I already had another draft ready for me to publish. I am so glad that I accidentally forgot about the first draft. This anthology you are holding in your hands is more intentional. Confessions gives a voice to pleas and issues that people wish they could say out loud. Hopefully, this poetry anthology will give you courage to speak your truth and eventually take whatever action needs to be done to make yourself and/or this world a better place.

I am thankful to my family and friends who have supported me over the years. Within the last two years of my author journey, the joy that exudes from my heart never ceases when my family members and friends make it a point to attend book fairs and performances. Extremely grateful for the family members, friends, and new family members (refuse to call you fans or patrons) who have purchased my books.

One of my biggest supporters is my mothers. Proud is an understatement when you hear, "Your mom [who was currently at the book fair] told me about you and your book." Support is love!

I also appreciate people who have given me a platform to speak life at their venues and events. Being entrusted to perform and lead poetry workshops is truly a blessing.

I would also like to give my flowers again to Jamal and Karen Washington who are also known as Bugsy Calhoun and Wintah Storm. Collectively, you have pushed me to become a better writer and performer. Seeing your faces in crowd at different performances warms my heart every single time.

When editing this book, I had to hire a new editor, who I glad we were writing sisters first. Sharon Morgan, I am greatly appreciative how you caused me to dig deeper with my poetry. I am always open and willing to learn and I know I grew as a writer because of you.

Table of Contents

Confessions	1
Grandparents Should Live Forever	4
Intercession	7
Neglected	10
Momma, What Are You Teaching Me?	12
Levels of Fatherhood: Part I, Absent	15
LIVE	17
Acceptance vs. Assignment	18
A Tribute to My Songbird	21
Avoiding the Label, Revisited	24
Hiding or Waiting	29
Hopeless	31
Clouded Euphony	33
Poetic Interpretation of Can't Let It Go by Jaime Woods	36
Peak Into the Game	39
Afraid of Forever	40
Breaking Shackles	43
Obstructions	45
Darkness	48
How Many?	50
Distress	52
You Ain't Saying Nothing	54
We Were Never Pawns	55
Where Are My Flowers?	57
Do You Know Me Enough to Teach Me?	61
Faithless Trying to Be Faithful	66
Monkey on My Back	68
Pray	71
HOPE	74

"Confessions"

Confessions…
Expressions
your heart beats
but won't escape
the false imprisonment
of your rib cage.

Confessions…
Messages
the soul boasts loudly.
Boldness is her footstool.
Determined to speak life.

Confessions…
Advice
cries softly.
Wishing for courage
or someone else to voice it.

Confessions…
Declarations.
Singing proudly
of the victories.
Rejoicing
in what is coming.

Confessions…
Secrets
never been divulged

despite desperation
for exposure.

Confessions . . .
Apology
never spoken
or bears repeating.
Still healing,
recovering.

Confessions . . .
Acknowledgement
certainty this road
I am traveling
is on the map of life
or admitting
I made a wrong turn
at the light.

Confessions . . .
Creeds
that speak of my belief.
Confirming my principles.
Unstoppable
I am.
You are too.

Confessions . . .
Atonement
Making it easy to share
past mistakes

in order for you
to avoid heartache.

Confessions . . .
Excuses,
Explanations
to help bring reason, clarity
into the equation.
Understanding the variable, the why.

Confessions . . .
Pleas
for you to listen
Maximize your gifts
Stop being foolish
Believe you are worth it.

Confessions . . .
Truths in need of a listening ear.
Who is willing to hear without judging?
Who is willing to hear and eventually do something?

"Grandparents Should Live Forever"

There is a prayer that is so unrealistic
    but I still believe God should hear it.
Hear my plea, a fantasy, a fairy tale.
I appreciate you listening to me.

Grandparents should live forever!

Crazy to hear but anyone who holds
    their matriarchs and patriarchs
    as the pinnacle of their affection
    would agree we should never part
    with the thread of our existence.

Forever we want to sit at their feet,
    listen to their wisdom.
Sitting in a kitchen that should only fit maybe ten
    but love allows more.
People are willing to sit on the floor,
    stand by the door
    captured by the stories,
    endless memories bringing tears of joy.

Front porches could either be silent,
    interrupted by a car horn, followed by a wave.
Sometimes it was a breath of fresh air
    to stare into God's country while again
    being engulfed in matters of the heart,
    overtaken by God's blessings!

Grandparents give kisses, hugs and warm plates of love
    saturating your soul,
    instilling wholeness,
      strengthened to conquer the unknown.

They should be able to bargain with God.
Say it is here I want to stay.
Whether it is 75, 80, 90 or 102,
    they would be able to inhabit this earth,
    witness more births, graduations, weddings and reunions.

They should want for nothing.
Never will they be tired or bothered.
No sickness or disease keeps them from experiencing abundance.
We would make sure every need is met.
Every want is fulfilled.
Thrilled they get to witness another generation
    covered in God's favor and their prayers.
Yes, they should be able to live to see their pleas to
    heaven manifest!

I know I sound foolish, selfish.
I would keep them here longer
    instead of with our Father.
I know the wisdom, recipes and stories
    flow through us like blood and water.
Every part of our entity,
    including our decision making,
    echoes your values and lessons in our psyche.
Stellar it would be to call them up.
Dialing up that 843 area code.

Driving down 26 to say I made it.
It took me long enough, but I listened.
Understanding God is the reason why I am living
Giving Him my attention to enables me to win and be a blessing.
A blessing who misses her blessings immensely!
A blessing who just wants her blessings here with me.
Desiring to see the pride on your face while witnessing
    your prayers manifesting.

Confessions

"Intercession"

It is not that I am hopeless.
Deep in darkness.
Hope refuses to exist.
Hiding in the shadows.
Traumatized by what lingers.
The rope that once dangled was burned
    by my anger, bitterness, sadness.
I can't rest.
The best has eluded me.
The worst has included me.
Imagination has turned into a nightmare.
Prayers don't seem to be answered.

Tears are filling the ocean of emotions.
Drowning any purpose.
Ultimately I feel deserted, worthless.
Comfortable with forsaking my right
    to pursue happiness.
There is no need for me to lie.
My belief isn't wavering.
Limp with stagnation, decaying.

Desperately need you to see through the ...
    I'M OKAY
    Maybe another day
    The missed phone calls
    Not caring at all
    Smiling while it hurts.
Burying myself slowly.

Desperately need you to . . .
    notice my clothes are dirty.
Desperately need you to . . .
    speak life into me.
Desperately need you to . . .
    unlock me from my prison.
Desperately need you to . . .
    raise me from this grave.
Don't wait another day
Don't ignore the signs,
    the closed captioning tormenting my soul.

Wholeness is what I crave under the layers of shame.
I lost my way.
Maybe you can send for Him.
Maybe you talk to Him.
Plead He sees me crying.
Appearing not to be hearing.
I don't know if He knows.

Consumed and overwhelmed,
    it is hard to tell if I am closer to heaven or hell.
You can be that repairer of the breach.
Reaching and pushing me back to the truth.
Abandoning the false notion,
    I belong here.
Steer me clear from the fear
    paralyzing, suffocating
    what little I assume I have left.
Not realizing little is much.
Little is enough.

Confessions page 9

Enough is much.
Help me see I am enough.
Beat down, torn to pieces.
You will revive the beauty, no ashes.
Only value and importance
    outweighing the despondence and disappointment.
Help me see it in me.

"Neglected"

I used to ride in the front seat.
Now restricted to this cramped space
   while he is laughing it up
   with the lady of my life.

I used to ride in the front seat.
Laugh with her.
Talk about my day.
Now stuck in the back,
   listening to their boring conversations.
No longer the center of attention.
Did she forget to mention she has a son?
Hey, I am back here.
At one time, I always sat up there.
Now she lets this joker come between us.

She says she is alone.
How is she lonely when I was here?

Did she forget?
   the nights I pretended the tears of pain were tears of joy.
   cuddles, warm blankets with cookies and milk
   comforting any loss or stress.

Did she forget?
   I used to bring her breakfast in bed:
   cereal, orange juice, and toast
   Too young to use the stove.

Did she forget?
   I gave her flowers out of the neighbors' yard.
   After all, she has always been my cheerleader.
   Sidelines were filled with her coaching, her presence.

Confessions

Concerts didn't end without her starting the standing ovation.

Did she forget?
    Family vacations were just with the two of us.
    Traveling to places we both enjoy.
    Now she brings him along, her boy toy.
    Couples retreat with a third wheel.
     I shouldn't feel this way.

I am so tired of riding in the backseat.
Wish she would notice me.
Stop giving him all the attention.
She shouldn't forget she has a son.
Her priority shouldn't be landing a new husband.

"Momma, what are you teaching me?"

Momma, what are you teaching me?

I cry because you cry.
You tell me to wipe my tears.
Sometimes I wonder whether or not
    you believe it will cause the rage to grow into an inferno.
This household is already consumed with his constant blaze.
Night after night...
Day after day...
I wonder why you continue to let him stay.
Praying God will see beauty in the ashes, the remnants lingering.
Surprising ourselves, we survive his venom.

Momma, what are you teaching me?

Is love supposed to feel this way?
Rainbows are always overpowered by hurricanes and
    tornadoes hailing down blows.
Nobody knows exactly how to forecast or predict.
How we wish we knew how to avoid
    the slaps, punches, kicks, and bruises,
      followed by excuses.
He must have missed that lesson in school
    when you are expected to breathe.
Sticks and stones should only build homes.
Alone they should not be allowed to soothe your ego
    while shattering bones.
The peace, joy, and solace we used to experience on a
    daily basis have been eradicated.

Confessions

Momma, what are you teaching me?

Your presence is the warm blanket;
    yet a trigger he grips relentlessly,
        unapologetic until you threaten to leave.
Bluffs, puffs of smoke that choke any glimmer of hope.
Deaf to your promises and fantasies he will change.
Why does he need to be given another opportunity
    not to prove himself worthy?
Supporting our family financially
    should never grant him permission,
    access to leave his signature,
    his handprint to disfigure,
        disgrace what God deemed beautiful.

Momma, what are you teaching me?

Once, I was fascinated with the color purple.
Now nauseated at the exquisiteness,
    constantly reminded of what seems to be a permanent stain
    from the hailstorm-swinging blows.
Fright should never be comfortable in your soul.
Fear and tension are a normal occurrence that
    shouldn't be mistaken for rainbows and sunshine.

Momma, what are you teaching me?

Is love supposed to feel this way . . .
Hand grenades overpowering hugs and kisses.
The ego stays tripping, screaming for healing.

Yet fixated on dealing with feelings by suppressing
    anything resembling affection.
Neglecting, abandoning adoration and admiration.
Harnessing an evil corrupting the hearts of those
    around him.
Never can I escape the images.
Ingrained in my psyche.
Behind closed eyelids, I see him.
I detest him.
Yet, all I see is him.
Bewitched into thinking this dysfunction,
    this chaos is a common place.
Dreams and fantasies morph into a reality,
    a nightmare I can't wake up from.
Sleepwalking into relationships mirroring,
    Momma, what you taught me.

"Levels of Fatherhood: Part 1 -- Absent"

Absent
Nonexistent

Refusing to be a father
caught up in
the dollar I deserve
to keep.
She ain't getting
nothing
from me.
My time is too precious
to invest in another
What can I truly offer?
You are better off
without me.
Failing to see
it is you
who suffers ultimately.

Absent
Irrelevant

Sometimes I desire to be there.
Yet, she is being selfish.
We couldn't make the relationship
valid or work.
She hides you from
 who can affect your future.

Lies are created
to deviate your
attention
from knowing me.

Absent
Nonexistent

A secret that must be hushed
Yes, it was us
who brought you here.
My family can't know,
on the down low.
Actually off the radar you must remain.
Can't disgrace my name,
my legacy can't
be tarnished, shredded
due to your existence.

Excuses
Cop outs
Evasions
Jive
Justifications
A song and dance
that will never
receive an encore from you.

Confessions

"LIVE"

I miss lying next to her.
I miss the warmth that would melt away the cold of the night.
The frights disappeared when
I could climb into her arms where I was safe.
The frights appear because she isn't here.

Lately, I have to go there
    where it is dark and cold.
Her bed used to be my sanctuary.
A getaway from norm.
Now it encompasses a storm.
Quiet, barely above a whisper.
Kissing her forehead good night.
Searching for her soul.
Eyes closed.
Sad because she refuses
    to fight for her life.
Her peace and happiness
    as hard as a brick
    constantly shattering my dreams
    she is coming back to me.
Hope is dangling.
I miss her singing me to sleep.
Stories with alternate endings.
I don't want a new beginning.
Just you to start living.

"Acceptance vs. Assignment"

I'm just a girl in the world trying to feel accepted.
I'm tired of being . . .
   neglected,
   rejected,
   told I'm not good enough.
I'm tired of saying I don't fit the mold.
I don't fit.
I don't fit.
I don't fit.
Nothing about me feels comfortable.
I just want to feel comfortable.
I want to be able to
   breathe in...breathe out
    without anyone criticizing me
   legislating how I wear my hair,
   the right to bare children,
   or snatch away my voice, my choice,
    judging and scolding how my hips switch or twerk,
   how they perfectly fit in jeans.
I mean...can I just be me without
    you bringing out the measuring stick?
    Placing me on scales to see how I
    compare to my sister.

I am just a girl in the world who just wants to be accepted.
I am tired of being
   neglected or rejected.
Priority is not the vibe you giving.
Shunned and used behind closed doors after late night texts.

Confessions

Conveniently and so easily you take from me.
My womanhood only appeals to your insatiable, lustful appetite.
My popularity gets you a seat at the table
    or in a photo op you can photo shop
    or finagle into your come up.
My soul suffers, my spirit is disrespected.
I'm tired.
Tired of being malnourished.
Needing to be fed, savored.

I'm just a girl in the world just trying to feel accepted.
Finally, I hear from heaven.
You are one of my greatest creations.
Wonderfully, woven together into a tapestry
    for the world to marvel and see.
Treasured and adored but never were you
    supposed to be the world's entertainment.
Never were you supposed depend on
    validation from people who didn't create you.
They don't understand the true value that is infinite.
From the beginning, you have been the object of my affection.
My thoughts towards you could never be counted by man
    like the endless grains of sand
    bordering the oceans and seas.
Man couldn't earn enough degrees to come up with a formula
    on how determine the number of hairs on your head
    that I knew from the start when you had my heart.
Faithfulness is my love language.
A stranger I am not, a friend I will always be present.
A powerful spirit embodying a loving father
    Who speaks fluently agape.

He reminds me
    I was never made to camouflage into society's norms.
Used to puzzle pieces fitting perfectly.
We assume we are to mirror that same ideology.
Nothing about our existence is supposed to blend in.
Masterpieces affirmed in destiny,
    reflecting the brilliant image of the creator.
Captivating the attention of many who stop to listen;
      wonder how they can too radiate an energy
      eliminating darkness.
Never caught up in the likes, hearts, followers, and subscribers
    when purpose, God's plan, is the only objective.
The royal priesthood who understood the assignment:
    excellence and being a blessing are never associated with
    congeniality.
Some may seem baffled at the plan.
Nevertheless, we don't waver.
Standing tall and ever abiding in the One
    Who has always welcomed me.
      Never rejected since I accepted His Son as my Savior.
      Forever covered, favored, a winner overtaken by blessings
      who doesn't need your acceptance.

Confessions page 21

"A Tribute to My Songbird"

You were my songbird.

The voice we all wish we could emulate.

Dancing in the mirror
desperately wanting
to convey the energy
radiated during your performances.

Watching your videos.

Never could quite hit a note like you
Never could hold a note like you.

Your smile melted the world
into one ear that refused to turn deaf to your gift.

Acting came naturally.
We exhaled with you.
Shed tears when you ran off the plane to meet him.
Connected as you tried to piece your marriage back
together with the preacher.

Adoration
was a crown
we gladly placed on you,
but easily snatched
when you didn't mirror
what we expected.

How quick
I mocked, ridiculed, scoffed
when you fell into temptation's grips.
Prayers were needed.
Understanding was never given.

"Crack is whack" caused us to laugh.

Again, why didn't I pray?
Why didn't we pray?
Encourage you to push through?
Instead, we tore down your mantle.
Destroyed your virtue.
Persecuted you, demanded you to bounce back
with all the daggers pointed at your heart.

You pushed through.
God enabled you.
Strengthened you.

Now you sing with the angels.

Absent from the body.
Present with the Lord.
Away from any naysayers.
Away from the pain,
constant shame.

Below, I am still deciding
if I want to believe
I will only be able to see you sing

through previous recordings.
No more interviews,
Red carpet debuts,
Guest appearances.

In my heart, I can only reminisce.

Deeply, I miss and wonder what else
I, we, could have done
to keep you here with us
longer.

Somber,
Your mother lost her only daughter.
Your brothers lost their only sister.
Your daughter lost her mother.

Comfort and peace, I wish for all.

Tears have yet to fall
but my heart mourns,
wishing I did more.
Realizing I can impact the world.
Live life to the fullest
Make choices that won't end the journey early.

Thank you for teaching me.

"Avoiding The Label -- Revisited"

Some would say we made the mistake
    of reading fairy tales to our daughters.
Happy endings mostly involving
    a prince coming to save her.
As to say she never had
    the power,
    the authority,
    the potential
    to stand alone without him.
Be, just exist, without him.
Be strong and powerful without him.
Sadly, those fairy tales has us thinking
    his presence is the only saving grace.
Some would say he is the missing puzzle piece
    to her wholeness.
Causing some to eventually
    dream, idolize, romanticize marriage
    as a needed rite of passage
    erasing inadequacies.

Realistically why are we the only gender
    who plan weddings, attires of the wedding party,
    and location of where we will jump the broom
    before we have fully bloomed.
While hoping for a bigger bra cup size,
    I would lie across my bed on Saturday morning
    reading my horoscope in the weekend editions of
    The State newspaper,
    the back of *Essence* Magazine,

Confessions

    mistakenly believing our sign will push
       father time to put me on his mind.

Shaking eight balls thinking this fluorescent cube
    will tell the truth of our love lives
The perfect picture etched with a pencil
    on a scratch piece of paper
    through games like MASH,
      hoping fate will have us with the mansion,
      husband, two kids and a fence enclosing
      us in this illusion of matrimony.

God intentionally created a woman.
Connecting her to man.
Never should we associate our purpose, wholeness, fulfillment
      with marriage.
We were created in the image of our Father
    Who says our existence is just enough.
Anything else added is a blessing,
      manifestations of abundant living not evidence of being.

Enthralled in saying yes to the dress, wedding story
    and any movie with the sappy typical ending.
Forgetting love already made her.
Love already saved her.
Caught up in expectations.
My timetable had me married by 25.
All three kids by 30.
Dismissing the author and finisher of the story.
Ignoring that it is an eternal commitment,
    not just a relationships status,

braggin' rights or topic of conversation.
A covenant that requires those to commit to be
   equipped, nourished, fulfilled,
     understanding that love is just scratching the surface.
I can't inhabit this space without substance.

I believe in the Creator of the universe and my destiny.
Yet entangled in fairy tales, misnomers, ideologies
   has me sitting across from this man who truly loves me.
The mood is enhanced with the candle lighting.
Enticing me
   in that moment to utter something I should feel for another.
However, entangled in my emotions,
   I can't admit this sentiment is genuine.
Reality is nonexistent.
Yet, in this moment, I am creating and molding a saying
   to fit what was never meant to be.
Casually, I let the music play.
The same tune you hear in the movies,
   the love stories, soap operas with the sappy ending.
"We belong together and you know that I am…"
No, I am not right.
This is all wrong.
Rewriting the script.
Professing I am in love
   not with the man God blessed me from above
   but with the feeling of being in love.
Being a part of a never-ending intimate embrace
Pretending my heart beats for you.
Willing to take this journey with you,
   a path unknown far away from my home.

Confessions

Destiny does not await me.
A plan etched since the beginning of time.
My creator warns me I have chosen to seek my own
    understanding.

Impatient --- tired of the clock ticking.
Willing to be what you want me to be.
Creating a false truth,
    I need your last name to put a period
    on this seemingly never-ending,
    run-on chapter of my life.
Being called someone's wife is the fulfillment I seek.
Tired of the sucking of teeth.
Followed by the fake laugh asking me,
"How come you ain't got no man?"
Willing to shout from the mountaintop.
Post pics on Instagram.
Change my status on Facebook.
Tag him on every picture so they can look and see.
Be proud of me.
Momma, aunty, cousins and homies,
    I didn't let another good man slip away.
None of them ask if I prayed for you.
No, they are just elated I stopped waiting.
Anticipating me saying, Yes, I do.
Ask God to bless this mess later.
Gotta escape the label of being alone.
Forcing a house to be a home.
Never built to last.
    Sinking in sand
        beneath the standard.

A standard sent down from Heaven with specific instructions.
Promises guaranteeing life more abundantly.
Yet, surely that doesn't apply to matrimony.
God is taking too long!
Blinded by all the wedding rings.
Seems that everyone has a boo thang expect me.
That one last train has stopped.
I am getting on without His permission.
I am missing God's best.
Faithless in the process.
Determined to avoid the label of being single.

"Hiding or Waiting"

Am I the only one
    who felt something deep in my soul
    when India Arie confessed she is ready for love?
She even had the audacity to question if love is hiding from her.
Finally, someone was recognizing what I felt deep down within.

Eventually, I realized my soul and heart
    were not speaking the same language.
It took years of heartache and mistakes to realize
    I can't identify with her sentiments.
That song is not my testimony, not my story.
Honestly, my reality is love is not looking for me.
For all I know, love is staring at me from across the room.
Nevertheless, it isn't willing to make a move.
He is waiting for God to orchestrate his steps.
Maybe he's just waiting on me
    to be everything that he needs me to be.
Am I the woman of God
    who pursues God with her whole heart?
Am I the woman of God
    whose purpose, her reason for living and being,
    is following the One Who
    created us to eventually be part of matrimony.

I cannot sit here and hope that he will find me,
    wonder if he's lost me if I've never found myself.
Do I know who I am?
Do I have what it takes?
What do I have to offer?

Is the list that I made comparable to what I can give?
The list I revisited after listening to Bill Winston,
    assuming my boldness will cause
    God to move him in my direction.
The only result is hearing a laugh from Heaven
    because the list wasn't an accurate representation
    of myself.

Again, love may not be hiding.
It could just be waiting for us to meet the requirements.
No, love isn't waiting for us to be perfect.
Nevertheless, you will be perfect for each other.
Why not give him everything I want from him,
    the best version of each other—
    two beings who are whole and healed?
I am not bringing any regurgitation of my past relationships
    into our situation.
I refuse to ruin a good thing.
I'm not trying to have him sitting on the roof,
    seeking to get away from the agonizing truth...
    that he should have just waited.

"Hopeless"

I know what it is like to be a hopeless romantic.
See my hope is misplaced in the hands of a man
    I pried open.
Forcing him to receive a dream
    he has never seen.
Our hearts aren't even in sync.
Somehow I fooled myself into thinking he is the one.
I pray to the Son to open his eyes to finally realize
    I am the one he is searching for.
Yes, I was hopeless.
Fantasizing what it would look like to be his bride.
Spending my life by his side to forever be framed as
    the perfect couple.
Ignoring that placing us together would cripple destiny.
A season giving mixed signals.
Spring with leaves fleeing to grass slowly decaying.
Desperate, just searching for someone to place a ring,
    symbolizing what is supposed to be so true and authentic.
A winter with snow chilling me to the bone
    yet beautifying what was lost.
I am marveling, but sadly panicking,
    rewriting the script filled with lies:
    he may be the only one who actually sees me.
Forgetting he doesn't even know me.
Destinies are not even intersecting.
Paths were never meant to cross.
Lost in desiring romance.
I want to give him a chance to
    play with my emotions,

  waste my time causing heartbreak.
I will blame him with the next one.
Omitting the detail that it was my fault:
  trusting in my own two cents with holes in them.

Confessions

"Clouded Euphony"

That was my song!
When it would come on I would . . .
    lean my head back.
    turn the radio up.
    close my eyes.
    scream "Aye, that's my jam!"
Speakers blasting.
Never mind dancing by myself.
Broom, mop or duster silently amplified my sentiments.
Didn't care if I was approaching my home.
Willing to roll past my house,
    a spin or two around the block, rocking to the rhythm.
Siting in the driveway while the harmonies left me enchanted.
Can't disturb this groove.
The radio can overplay it.
People can be tired of hearing it.
Eventually, the radio very rarely plays it.
A faint memory from the billboard chart.
Number one hit to my soul.
Never did it get old.
Seemingly, never retiring the repeat button on my playlist.

Then something shifts with your presence.
Strutting onto the stage, seemingly, on cue.
Singing the same melody.
Grooving while silently inviting me to rock with you.
Obliging.
Intrigued.
Seeking to feel your heartbeat.

Are we in sync?
Harmonizing?
Ignoring the discord.
Overlooking the broken track
The record is scratched.
The tape ribbon is pulled out.
The CD is skipping.
Eventually, the composition changed.
Foreign.
It doesn't belong to me.
Tied to the fantasy of being desired by you.
Good vibes linger.
Confusing lyrics hover,
    haunting every hook, verse, vamp.
Harmony is intertwined in your fragrance.
A hypnotic beat numbing me to the toxic lyrics.
Lacking substance.

Hate the first thought of you is attached to my song.
My song transfigured into our song.
Resuscitating ominous memories.
Forcing me to flash back when I just want to move forward.
Close the chapter.
Never wondering what could have been done differently.
No closure needed.
Fully aware the duet was a one-time performance.

Yet, I am still mad.
Your stench is still permeating the track.
Snatching it from my hit list, the ultimate playlist.
Pressing skip or changing the station.

Confessions

Lingering in the air, choking life.
Struggling to breathe, my chest tightens.
How stupid could I be
    to naively believe it should have worked?
Maybe I am just upset.
I invested time, my heart, in a collaboration
    with someone who was never meant to perform on the set.
Future collaborations weren't in the contract.
The chemistry was fleeting.
I refuse to stay entrapped by guilt.

Lost in an unknown beat.
Desperate to change the rhythm.
Forgetting my purpose isn't linked to you.
My verse wasn't written for you.
My beat, my dance was never for you.
Until my heart forgets, I can't listen to my song.

"Can't Let It Go" by Jaime Woods
(a poetic interpretation)

Today I realized I was out of my mind
    to indulge in my pride.
Preferring being right over doing right.
A point to be proven, made significant.
Weightless when I remember my vows.
Must drown out and stop obliging the naysayers.
Consuming unwise counsel from people
    who aren't Biblical, inexperienced.
Foolish to listen when there is no evidence of fruit.
Aloof, I let the distance grow between us.
Now I am cognizant of my misjudgment.
The answer to my prayer.
There is no other solution.
I can't ruin this union.
No one is supposed to come between
    what God joined together as one entity.
Here I am humbly admitting

I just can't let it go.
I just can't let it go.
I just can't let it go.

From the beginning,
    there was never an exit strategy.
We entered into this covenant
    convinced God created me for you.
I am your good thing.
Favored by God.

Confessions

Our destiny has a greater purpose.
Outweighing any mistreatment or hurt feelings.
Yes, we acknowledge and correct.
Never are we allowed to quit.
This is more than just I love you.
Two complete souls helping each other grow.
A calling to be an example, expanding the kingdom.
Wedding rings solidify the never ending circle.
Unbreakable.
Impenetrable.
A promise to honor and cherish.
For better or worse.
Richer and poorer.
Sickness and health.
It doesn't matter what life has dealt.
We forfeit the right to bow out
    when at the altar we said we are all in.
Despite my family thinking I am crazy not to leave,
    I will remember to trust in the One Who gave you to me.
Through Him we are strengthened.
Through Him we are renewed.
Through Him we are empowered
    to overcome this hardship,
    this momentary affliction
    that will never outweigh
    the glory from Heaven and our testimony
    we couldn't...
    you couldn't...
    I couldn't...
    we wouldn't
    let go.

I just can't let it go.
You just can't let it go.
We just can't let it go.

"Peak into the Game"

Can I waste your time?

Playing with your mind?
Putting you on a high that will soon die.
Moving on to the next chick.
Foolishly she will let me exploit her innocence.
Tarnish her value.
When I am tired of sexing her,
    she'll receive the same treatment.
I will stop calling, acknowledging
   I ever knew her.

Sadly, you will still be
    trying to reach me.
Wanting to know why I left.
Girl, you're type is so needy.
Busy waiting on a man to
    love you...
    save you...
    accept you...
    marry you.
Setting yourself up for failure.
All my kind wants to do is abuse the goods.

You do not realize you are precious and sacred.
Better discover your worth.
Then you will stop settling for guys who will treat you like dirt.

"Afraid of Forever"

He said he was afraid of forever.
Immediately, I wanted to snap back to that 25-year-old me
    who would say it's cool or whatever.
We don't have to rush this forever.
We can just be in the moment.
Momentarily buying time to change his mind about forever.
How clever we women think we are not realizing
    no man will commit to what is not in his heart.
How we allow our mind, heart, and soul
    to be torn apart by happiness –
    satisfied to be in the company of someone.
Yet, neglecting the memory of discontentment,
    the uneasiness of the connection.
You turn caution lights and detour signs into speed bumps.
Running through red lights, risking my life.
Forgetting some heartbreak is avoidable.
Changing direction.
No longer joyriding, lavishing in a fantasy unnaturally
    morphing into aggravation and frustration.

Who am I to pretend that what we were to each other
    was mutual?
Can't allow attraction to pervert my perception.
Yes, I won't ignore my intuition and experience.
Being whole and healed won't allow you to revel in foolishness.
My 42-year-old self is fully awakened to my worth.
Too wealthy to come off needy and greedy,
    begging for someone to give when it should be given freely.
I'm not here to convince him of what it should be.

Confessions

I am aware of our reality.
I'm not going to sit here and create a fantasy.
The truth is he's afraid of marriage.
I'm believe wholeheartedly in matrimony.
Two souls uniting as one.
Together we will journey under the sun
    while the One who brought us together
    will make us stronger,
      impacting generations,
      creating nations to follow.

I believe in everlasting love.
Enduring from yesterday through tomorrow.
Persevering from the past to the future.
Building with someone who God said he is your one.
When he said I am afraid of forever, in that moment,
    I realized I could never again in my life be that 25-year-old self.
Why divert back to my old self
    who tried to ignore the cards I was dealt?
Calling for a possible
      when doubt has caused me to be sandbagging books.
Disillusioned,
    believing I could make him look into my heart,
      influencing his psyche
    when all I did was fall again into more anguish.
Maturity allows me to clearly hear what he says.
I'm not trying to make him think or feel anything differently.
It is what it is.
I'm going to go on about my business.
No longer getting caught in my feelings.
Objectifying my emotions with abusive patterns.

My heart matters.
My soul weighs value.
I won't belittle you because you don't want to say I do.
I won't belittle myself because you don't see forever in me.
Happily, peacefully, I will wait for what I deserve.
Those lessons will turn into mistakes.
Remembering the heartache.
Vowing to no longer pretend.
Just know your words placed you in the friend zone.
No benefits to be reaped.
No showpiece or plus one to the parties.
Not even waiting until you are not afraid.
Leaving myself open.
Someone will envision forever with me.
No hesitancy, his heart is willing to see if our rhythm is in sync.
I deserve a man who is sure about me.
I deserve a king to reign with this queen.
As a result, saying I love you for now and eternity.

Confessions

"Breaking Shackles"

Refused to stay locked up in the cage.
Breaking the shackles.
Surprisingly, my mind isn't in shambles.
Witnessing my brothers swing from trees.
I must escape their inability to see me as a man.
Resilient, seeking rest from the war.
Pressing on . . .
    mentally, physically equipped
    to continue to build this country for my family.
No more will you take the credit and not acknowledge me,
    the pillars this country stands on.
The force who refuses to move on without justice,
    life and the pursuit of happiness.
I have rights: I won't stand idly while you deny them.
Freedom isn't just the dream of my ancestors.
It is the reality of kings and queens
    who did then and now rule the earth.
Snatching back my identity from those who still seek to
    oppress me,
    silence me,
    annihilate me.
Never mind whether I am in the south, north, east or west,
    forever fighting through red lines,
    the morphing of racism into policies and laws.
Refusing to allow the walls to cave in.
Refusing to give in.
Refusing to accept this is just how it will be.
I must escape their inability to see me as a man.
Resilient, seeking rest from the war.

Pressing on . . .
Mentally, physically equipped
    to continue to build this country for my family.
I have rights: I won't stand idly while you deny them.
Freedom isn't just the dream of my ancestors.
It is the reality of kings and queens
Who did then and now rule the earth.
Creating spaces.
Taking opportunities and sitting in rooms
    while exposing the truth of your bigotry,
        challenging and changing your definition of American citizens.
No longer can we give our allegiance
    to the obliteration of our essence, our being.
We deserve, we demand, freedom, equity
    that isn't the dream of my ancestors.
It is the reality of kings and queens
    who by any means will overcome
        the blatant disregard of our humanity.

Confessions

"Obstructions"

My view was obstructed.
Flag was removed.
Yet the monuments still stand with pride, laughing,
    mocking our attempt to reclaim our identity as
    superior beings.

We thought the war would end it.
The president never intended to grant us freedom.
Only victory for the union.
Secession would ruin his legacy.

Unrealistic expectations, we would be seen as equals.
We never asked for a seat at the table.
We had our own table snatched away,
    commanded we serve and build tables for people
    we have to fight for the right to sit at the table
    we constructed.

Deemed our complexion darkness
    When our melanin shines brighter than any star.
    Our hue is impenetrable.

Rebirth
Reborn.
We have weathered the storm
Through every period and era of struggle.
    Slavery.
    Confederacy.
    Reconstruction.

Hamburg Massacre.
Jim Crow.

Impossible.
Unstoppable.
Unpopular until profitable.
Robbed and misappropriated.
Mimicked and manipulated.

Thank God some of us are awakened or
    were never sleeping.
Aware our eminence has existed
    since the beginning of time.
The same God you claim is also ours, mine.
Had us all in mind.
Yet, we are separated because some of you
    continue to perpetuate a system, rooted in hate.
Monuments obstructing my view of justice.
Blocking anti-lynching laws.
Indignantly and violently opposing our rights to vote.

We will continue to proclaim, declare and demand
    change must and will take place.
The removal of the flag wasn't enough.
Monuments, statues of hate have been grounded in
    other states.
We must join the rally cry.
Emerging is a new identity of this country
    who loves all its citizens.
Not just when it is convenient like chanting team USA
    during the Olympics.

Confessions

Can't pledge allegiance.
We were never one.
We can no longer lie:
    this country wasn't made for you and me.
Forced to be here.
We are aware you never intended to accept
    our presence as nothing more than subservient.
Domination was the only language you spoke.

You will be forced to recognize the truth.
We were always on your level, if not higher.
Never once did we seek revenge.
Only seeking to tear out the pages of *your* textbooks.

The same people who have been tenacious, courageous.
Strengthened while rising above
  the false teachings our lives never mattered.
Our hope will never shatter.
Indestructible in the midst of seeing our kings and queens
    swing from trees.
Fleeing burning towns we built.
Yes, our faith is bullet proof
    despite the unaccounted for and wrongful death lawsuits.
The message is clear but we ain't hearing nothing
    that doesn't esteem our rights to freedom.
Dismantle the trophies of hatred.
Exhume the sacred ground of bigotry.
Only true heroes deserve to stand carved in stone.

"Darkness"

Tonight I felt a cold darkness seeking to poison my soul.
Forgetting God has everything under control.
As grief grips my heart...
As I glare at every mother's nightmare,
   their seed lying there lifeless
     under the white sheet not representing its meaning,
   denying my son everything.
They didn't see my son pure without malice.
Immensely harmless, yet they found my boy to be a threat.
His skin frightened you.
Deemed hostile.
No way this child, this man, has any goodness in him.
Wicked and evil you are.
Sadly, the never-ending story will eventually be spoken
    by media who will seek to disgrace his name.
Suppress or erase the memory of a king in the making.
No, there is no celebration so this sheet should be black,
    lacking humility.
You can't be honest and admit your soul was up for hire.
You along with the rest never protect us.
Never fair when someone with lighter skin
    lives to see another day.
Lacking a sense of community and integrity.
Blinded by your fear of every black man or woman you see.
My child was golden.
Academics were going to pay for college!
Dreams of building me a house.
His future spouse, whoever she was,
    would forge a connection

bringing me grandkids,
building a legacy
snuffed out by your ignorance.

"How Many?"

How many bodies have to be lowered to the ground
    for us to propel past the alarm?
Too many of us have pressed the snooze button.
Allowed the pillow to shut out
    the agonizing screams wailing for help.

How many bodies have to lay flat, bleeding into the ground
    like it is normal, natural as fertilizer and water?
How many others must mourn the untimely, illogical death
    of daughters, sons, brothers, mothers and fathers?

How many bodies have to fall all because
    we have cowards who are afraid to legislate, mandate
    not everybody has the right to carry?
Not everyone has the mental capacity to know
    what is reality or fantasy.
How many dreams must turn into nightmares?

How many deaths are too many?
How many mass murderer stories must run across the screen
    before we are awakened from this coma?
We are numbed to the point of not caring
    enough to change law.

We can't, won't be silent.
We must vote people out.
We must vote people in.
We hold them accountable.
We must attend meetings and briefings

ensuring the law reads what it needs to say.
We can't let the gun manufacturers have their way.
We can't let them have a say in who lives and who dies.
We understand the value of life.

We understand the value of life.

"Distress"
Inspired by the Netflix movie adaptation
of **MONSTER** by Walter Dean Myers

I brace myself.
Clenching my blouse.
Maybe they won't hear my heart beating so loud.
Maybe I can stop it from bursting,
    breaking from grief.
My baby has been stolen from me,
    swallowed whole by the streets.
God can only deliver him like
    Jonah from the whale of the sea.
Never was he running from purpose.
He embraced it.
Thrived in it.
Yet, his value has been stripped, demeaned,
    equated with juvenile delinquents,
    repeated offenders blind to promise.

Gripping my shoulder like hope is strapped to my chest.
In desperate need of comfort,
    begging my father in heaven to bring him home.
He's not where he belongs.
He is not the name they smear on his reputation.
Integrity, innocence locked up due to a lapse in judgment.
Guilty by association,
Guilty before proven faultless,
    shouldn't be excuses to feed the belly of injustice.

Despite being bombarded by the pressure of this world

    to be a heartless cruel thug,
He has always embraced his true heritage, his lineage --
    his brilliant eminence.
Understanding his assignment,
      capturing the world with his lens.
Now hoping he won't get trapped in the system.
They call it justice.
Designed to stagnate, eliminating the threat to the majority
      who they deem to be the only pillars of society.
Forgetting we are the builders of this country.
We just want to be seen, not devalued.
Embracing our truth.
We are human too.

"You Ain't Saying Nothing"

Ain't nobody in prison
    bragging about the bars that hold them hostage
    while making a profit.
Billions of dollars are earned from lost souls.
Capitalizing off Kings and Queens who misconstrued, squandered
    their power.
Lacking knowledge or the awareness of their potential.
Ain't nobody in jail or any prison cell
    boasting about hell is the best place to be cool.
Fool is what they would shout to me and you,
    your brother and your cousin, too.
Stripped of humanity.
Restricted to confinements.
Normalcy prohibiting productivity.
Stagnation is the stench clouding senses into believing
    the cycle can't be broken.
Yes, we cry, fight for falsely arrested and unjustified sentences.
Yet stand perplexed…baffled…flabbergasted…
As some gaslight a lifestyle you will see after while
    only fattens the pockets of the greedy
    who never truly seek to rehabilitate.
Systems and media capitalize off the lies
    bringing demise mostly to our communities.
Only snuffing out Kings and Queens
    who make the mistake of trading their castles for cell blocks.

Confessions

"We Were Never Pawns"

We can't get used to this.
I feel like some of us have accepted
    this is just the way it is.
Countless headlines of another baby being snuffed out
    by violence.
Images stupefying our senses, silencing our cries.
Failing to question God why,
    too paralyzed by grief
    to seek answers on how we can put a stop to this.
There is a demand to be cognizant,
    aware our kings and queens
    are being duped into behaving like pawns
    carrying out the devil's plans
    to neutralize and annihilate powerful beings
    who were solely created to reflect greatness.

Our ancestors built and ran kingdoms.
Established civilizations admired by many nations.
Even after being kidnapped and enslaved,
    we've found a way to escape,
    evading the mental prison
    poisoning us to believe we weren't supreme.
By any means, we adapted and created a road map to freedom.
Building cities and towns
    despite them burning them down.
They did not erase our progress.
We define perseverance.
Professions we have perfected . . .
    Government officials,

Teachers,
Lawyers,
Doctors,
Rappers,
Designers,
Engineers.

Some want to choke out dignity and integrity,
    recklessly endangering lives over pride.
A mother should only have her face drenched in tears
    due to being overjoyed by her baby's accomplishments.
They should never fall into his or her casket.
Inconceivable, unfathomable.
Nevertheless, we must remain hopeful
    with what seems out-of-control.
This darkness must reveal a glory so radiant and
    magnificent we can only testify God did it.
Manifested His deity through His body, His people
    who never got used to it
    who never gave into it
    who reclaimed the village
    who never forsook the calling
    reminding our kings and queens
    who they are
    who they were always destined to be:
    royalty.

Confessions

"Where Are My Flowers?"

In the beginning of the pandemic,
    panic and chaos exposed fears, failures and truths.
No one knew how this disease would
    rip another normal ideal into shreds.
Churches, schools and places we frequented
    were seldomly visited out of the fear of COVID.
In the midst of panic and uncertainty,
    I refused to lose my sanity.
Every now and then I would breathe relief.
A sign that would bring joy, a hope of a brighter tomorrow.
Connecting to my students through a screen.
It seemed that parents finally understood.
Parents were finally singing our, teachers', praises.
Parents said we deserved raises all because
    they had to teach their own children.

Complaints could build a skyscraper to heaven.
How in the world do you, we, teach
    a class of sometimes 20, 30, or 40
        different personalities and capabilities?
The struggle was real with your one, two or possibly four.
Now all of sudden you adorn us with a crown
      as the greatest profession
      and a cape for being the superhero
      who has battled through every villain unimaginable.
You make promises to never forget
    another Teacher Appreciation Week.
You make promises to support the teacher's

needs and wants to just to truly feel valued.

Well, can I be honest with you?
We're still waiting on our flowers.
It is October and we ain't trying to wait on April
    to bring showers that spring forth May flowers.
Teacher Appreciation Week means nothing
    if we don't have the resources and peace
    to be the greatest profession
    that has been more than just a blessing but a conduit of magic.
We are the great conductors who orchestrate this world to spin.
No, I am not saying we are God.
We are definitely His creations who took on His calling to impact
    knowledge, guidance that empowers
    your children to be a prosperous generation.
Yes, we impact nations.
Yet, you want to handicap our lessons by creating standards
    demanding that we erase history.
You want to empty bookshelves of the books
    that only reflect your ideology.
Anything contradictory gets banned and burned.
Freedom of speech is only given to the school board members
    who have hidden agendas to reflect
    what they believe is the greatness of this country.
The legacy of eradicating anything
    that doesn't reflect domination of any nation.
A land already inhabited by Native Americans.
A land built by enslaved Africans.
A land we were indoctrinated to sing songs about how it was ours.
Never seemed to reap anything but scraps
    you didn't want from the harvest we planted.

Confessions

Again, I ask where are our flowers?
Pay raises are just a small portion of the bouquet.
What about enough sick days to cover unexpected illnesses
    or just needing a day to recover mentally?
Why don't you add administration
    who supports the heartbeat of the school?
They are willing to fight policies pushing
    more gifted beings into other professions.
They are tired of being overwhelmed and under pressure.

We would also like parents who know we are here to serve,
    reemphasizing what has already been learned.
We are humans who want what is best.
Please allow grace to proceed from your lips
    before you are quick to attack,
      shoot daggers you never take back or
    ask to help bandage the wounds you caused.
Ultimately, we need all of you to collectively hear our plea.
Actually do something like vote!
Bring the same attendance you do during Friday nights
    to the poll, SIC, PTO, and school board meetings.

We can't keep watching the institution crumple
    then patch it up scotch tape and glue sticks.
We are sick of sitting in the nosebleed sections
    while legislations create more problems,
      I mean policies only catering to a minority.
The whole faculty just wants to be valued for doing
    what you could never do effectively,
    which is to cultivate our babies into leaders

who will hopefully want to be teachers
because they witnessed their heroes
finally receiving their capes.

Confessions

"Do You Know Me Enough to Teach Me?"

Inspired by the book written by Stephen G. Peters
Do You Know Enough about Me to Teach Me: A Student's Perspective

Do you know me enough to teach me?

Reach me through the bars?
The wounds are scars
    weighing heavy on my mind and heart.

Yet you want me to . . .

Focus on me learning math—
    some call it arithmetic,
    science, history, English.
Put punctuation at the end of the sentence.
Capitalize the word at the beginning.
Forgetting I can't lower case or erase my upbringing.

You worried about test scores.

I am constantly fighting my peers
    who clown how my mom feeds us.
Many knock on the door.
I don't call them uncles anymore.
Ashamed but will not back down
    from defending her name.
Always get blamed.
They don't hear the words stabbing me.

Never do you seek understanding.

Fear is normal and my mom is too blind to see.
Something about him supporting us financially
    makes it okay to be used as his punching bag.
I don't need another dad.
I would like to be happy in my home, not sad.
Defensive because we don't know what will set off
    this man who resembles an explosive.

A man at home because either pops was never there or
    he got shipped off again to fight a war
    tearing my world apart.
Some call it babysitting.
If we are honest, it is borderline parenting.
Cooking dinner, keeping the house cleaned.
Doing my part and making sure the younger ones eat.
Helping with their homework.
Then putting my siblings to sleep
    after praying for our God to keep by bringing help, relief.
Sleep deprived while mom works at night
Next morning we start again.
Fixing breakfast, getting ready for school.
Late again and you want to enforce the rules
Being expected to act a part I forgot to play.

Again, you want me to . . .

Focus on learning math—
    some call it arithmetic,
        science, history, English.

Confessions

Put punctuation at the end of the sentence.
Capitalize the word at the beginning.
Forgetting I can't lower case or erase my upbringing.

A house with no lights.
Cabinets are bare.
You would never know by the purse mama totes.
Flashy, she makes sure my sister and me
    resemble a fantasy.
All is good.
Life is great.
In reality, we are hungry.

Choking on my own vomit.
I am his playmate.
Daddy, these games make me feel violated.
Trudging to school the next day where I am safe.
Where I can rest so I place my head on the desk.
No, I don't need to see the nurse.
Just want to sleep in the only place I can find rest.

Yet, you want me to . . .

Focus on me learning math—
    some call it arithmetic.
    Science, history, English,
Put punctuation at the end of the sentence
Capitalize the word at the beginning.
Forgetting I can't lower case or erase my upbringing.

Acting out is the only way

I get noticed.
Yelling serves no purpose.
I am numb to the repetition of the lack of affection.
Does anyone really see me?
Need to be feeling wanted, valued.

Try something different.
Compliment my hair, dress, or shirt.
Make a fuss when I am absent.
Don't care if you're lying.
At least you are trying to melt my ice box.
Tell me I am intelligent.
See past my mess and into my potential.
Sometimes you forget we are just children,
      finding our way, carving a path.
If it is crooked, help me straighten it.
Lead me in the right direction.
Call my parents, tell him how I improved.
My half glass just needs some of you to make it full.

Then I will be able to…

Focus on me learning math—
    some call it arithmetic,
    science, history, English.
Put punctuation at the end of the sentence
Capitalize the word at the beginning.
Forgetting I can't lower case or erase my upbringing

It won't be a hindrance or an excuse.
I have the ability to choose.

Confessions page 65

I excel because of someone who knows me.
Someone who cares for me.
Knows me enough to teach me.

"Faithless trying to be Faithful"

I have a man who loves and adores me.
He gave His life for me.
He would move Heaven and earth to make me smile.

Yet, I keep foolishly running back to him...
him who despises his love for me,
him who will do anything to lure me
    away from the Lover of my Soul,
        him who doesn't even love me,
            but only cares about keeping us apart.

I see past his mischievous plan.
I go back to the One whose arms are always open.
Ready to forgive.
Willing to forget me being unfaithful.
Forever He is faithful to His promise to love me.

Despite knowing Who is best for me,
I find myself being seduced again and again
Away from the only true love I will ever know,
Enticed by the one who just wants to
    weaken me,
    abuse me,
        keep me from living out my destiny.
Bruises and scars on my heart.
Joy is nonexistent in my soul.
Temporary happiness that quickly turns into sadness
    when I realize he has never been right for me.

Confessions

After feeling constant disappointment in hearing
    that my life will be better with him,
       I can no longer be naive to the lies he fed me.
Attempting to bamboozle me into believing
    my Love will never take me back again.
He wants me to believe
    He will never forgive and forget me breaking His heart again.
Mistakenly believing my mistakes outweigh scriptures saying
   The faithful love of the Lord never ends.
   His mercies never cease.
   Great is his faithfulness;
   His mercies begin afresh each morning.
My spirit brings these words of life back to my remembrance.
My Love senses I desire to be back in His presence.
He assures me I have and will never have nothing to worry about.
He is never changing.
His love is always remaining, inviting me back home.
Insisting he will never stop loving me.
Causing me to return to Him again determined to never leave.

"Monkey on My Back"

There's this monkey on my back.
Not a knapsack with the imprint of a cute fuzzy face.
There's this monkey on my back.
You refuse to erase my shame.

My father has engraved my name in blood in the book of life.
He told me what I have done that wasn't right
    has been erased forever.
Never to be remembered.
Never to be brought up again.
Yet, you continue to condemn.
Now there's this monkey on my back.

You refuse to erase my shame.
You refuse to let my name come out of the mud.
Maybe you are just mad.
Determined to stop any other shine.
Maybe you believe you are stuck.
Determined to keep me in that same place,
    regret and stagnation associated with disgrace.
Not realizing I am not fazed by your opinions of me.

This monkey on my back you see
    is just another obstacle, hurdle
        attempting to distract me.
Refused to be focused on you.
Focused on Him
      who believes I am eternally righteous,
      which means there is nothing

able to blemish or tarnish my image in Him.
I am a new creation in Him.
Enabled to receive everything He has for me.
Unstoppable,
> even with this monkey on my back.

I am still able to achieve and conquer anything.
This monkey is lightweight.
I am strengthened in Him to overcome everything

Go ahead and live in yesterday.
I am living in today.
Pressing towards my future.
I refuse to be burdened in what should be shared as a testimony,
> helping others to be set free.

Hopefully, you come along with me.
Travel with me to live this abundant life
Instead of focusing on
How is she living like that?
Forgetting when she used to do this and that
I used to go to the clubs with her and I used to drink with her
Puff puff pass with her
I used to . . .
Well, we had some other situations that will go unheard.
If the walls could speak . . ."

You wish they could speak.
Nevertheless, I will answer your questions.
I realized my flesh was weak.
No longer can I depend on myself.
In Him I must live, move and have my being
No longer a slave to sin.

Conquering through Him.
Never letting go of His love and grace.

Losing this monkey you try to use to bind me.
Rebuked in Jesus' name.
There is no shame.
Grace and mercy have been covered.
Pushing me to always abound in the One
    Who lives in me,
    Who died for me,
    Who keeps me holy,
    and keeps you questioning

    How is that the same girl who used to roll with me?

Confessions

"Pray"

**My mother prayed for me.
She had me on her mind.
She took the time to pray for me.
I'm so glad she prayed.
I'm so glad she prayed.
I'm so glad she prayed for me.
The preacher...
My grandmother...
My father...**

My Father, why haven't I spoken to my Father?
Why has my Father, my God heard the pleas from another?
Why haven't I bothered to pray when
    I was the one who confessed that He is my Lord and Savior?
He is the one I believe was sent to sacrifice His life.
Crucified, shed blood that should have been my own.
Alone He bore the weight that I couldn't carry.
Buried then descended into hell's trenches.
Risen, resurrected into Heaven where He is King.
The King I believe is Christ, the Holy One, the powerful One.

So why haven't I prayed?
Prayed to the One Who I know fearfully and wonderfully
    handcrafted me.
The One Who saw fit to see that I come into this earth,
    be part of the purpose and the plan to set forth his kingdom.
I need to believe in the One
    Who knew me from the beginning of time?
    Who am I not to take the time to say thank you?

I need to pray.
I need to pray,
I need to pray.
Sit and listen to the instructions of the Lover of my soul,
    Who I say my life He holds.
Truly I must surrender, allow Him to have control.
Believing in His promises means I have to open up the Book.
Meditate, trust and believe all that He has for me.

I don't have to rely simply on the prayers of
    my mother, my father, my grandmother.
The prayers of the righteous availeth much.
That scripture shouldn't be my excuse to just fly on the wings of
    my mother's prayers.
He said he will always be there.
Omnipresent, He is everywhere.
Faithful, He calls me friend
My confession should be evidence of a relationship --
    a connection that will cause
    an outpour of blessings overtaking me
    abiding with my King.
Mother's, father's, grandmother's prayers should only carry me
    temporarily, pivot me into being there for my own salvation.
Seeking my Father first,
    His kingdom should be my focus, my mission.
Missing nothing because everything will be added, nothing lacking.
Something hits different when
    it is my mustard seed that harvested abundance
    that will keep producing, yielding.
Yes, the windows of Heaven stay open.

Confessions

Fellowshipping with my Shepherd and Provider.
Worshiping and praising, being engulfed in His presence;
    not another podcast or another life coach.
Better is one day in your courts than a thousand elsewhere.
Only need to stare and be aware of what God has for me.
Only need to trust in the Author and Finisher of my destiny.
The blueprint, He illustrated.
With Him, I can navigate the life He orchestrated for me
    to participate in and always win.

**Somebody Prayed For Me* by Dorothy Norwood

"HOPE"

I have a confession to make.
Once upon a time
    I couldn't justify the relevancy of
    being a devoted Christian.
Selfish, just trying to make it into Heaven.
Foolishly believing this gift was only meant for me.
Not realizing the greatest gift we give

Is to live a life drawing more unto Him.
In addition . . .
    carnal was my thinking.
I kept seeing Christians who are supposed to be victorious,
    losing.
Mistakenly, I believed holiness granted immunity or invisibility
    from tragedy and turmoil.
Obviously, I wasn't awakened to my authority or fully equipped
    with the knowledge of scriptures like
    For everyone born of God, overcomes the world.
    Everything works for the good of those who love him.
    For He knows the plans He has for me, which are to prosper
    me and not to harm me, plans to give me a hope and a
    future.
    My afflictions are momentary and don't compare to the glory
    that will unveil a testimony, a story, a song I will sing all day long
    praising our savior who delivered me from another one.

Know that I am now a mature Christian
    who has come to the realization of my experiences of Him.
I have continued to taste and see

Confessions page 75

    the Lord is more than good to me.
Grace and mercy follow me.
Awaking me every morning!
I can't allow the heaviness of these afflictions
    to cause me to start tripping, forgetting, and not believing in the
God who cannot lie, fail or deny Himself.

Can't deny the weight of the burden.
There is no comfort in it.
Yet, I am comforted and encouraged
    by another inscription on my heart.
I cast all worries and any anxiety on Him.
Keeping my mind stayed on Jesus, the One who strengthens me.
Infuses me with joy.
Wrapping me up in a peace,
    because I don't have to understand what is going on around me.
I don't have to know what is next on this journey.
The Author and Finisher of my faith says
    He will not withhold no good thing.
His daughter who is called according to His purpose.
Called according to His purpose doesn't mean I don't get nervous.
Doesn't block out the darkness.
Some days and nights you can't see.
Some days and nights you can't hear.
What I just described is the definition of faith --
    the assurance of things hoped for, the conviction of things not seen.

Yet, as a Christian, I have lived long enough I can rehearse the past
    victories revealing the undeniable character of God.
Never changing, all powerful and knowing.
Reminding and confirming deliverance or the ability to stand.

Overcoming is my outcome.
He's already won.
Saying *it is finished* covered any circumstance.
Igniting a fire and authority to speak life and death to anything
    that is happening.
Loosening and binding on earth as it is in Heaven.
I will not pretend like the outcome
    always plays out as I intend it.
I can't forgot that God is sovereign.
Things may not always turn out the way I expect them to.
That's why I have to keep pushing my way through,
    praising my way through,
    worshiping my way through
Despite looking surrounded, again, I am reminded that I am
    surrounded by Him, Jehovah Jireh.
He is always enough.
Grace is sufficient.
Let the world keep looking, anticipating.
David said he will make a table in the midst of my enemies.
Afflictions giving them a front row seat, witnessing the glory,
    a testimony, a story they will sing all day long about our Savior,
    now their Savior, causing them to experience
    the favor that lasts a lifetime.

All problems, despair, hardships have an expiration date.
Can't let my thoughts get stuck in a place
    where the coldness seeks to snuff out the warmth of His Word,
    where the storm stalls, seeking to silence any joy
    with thunder and lightning.
The guaranteed certainty there is a silver lining --
    promises that will outshine the aftermath.

Confessions

Surrendering all, which includes my thought patterns.
What I think matters.
Only seek to inhabit a space of resilience despite how I am feeling.
My feelings and circumstances don't negate the fact that
> God's love, mercy and grace are unfailing, unwavering, never
> ceasing, forever covering.

His favor is a shield.
My guide, my protection.

Despite the weapons being formed
> when that child I prayed for is a stillborn.
> when the parent you prayed for
> doesn't experience healing here on earth.
> when addictions among family members want to convince you
> the devil is in control . . .
> when poverty seeks to take up permanent residency
> choking any hope of breathing again.

Weapons can form but they are never prospering.
I keep confessing.
I keep believing.
We are hard pressed on every side, but not crushed;
> *perplexed, but not in despair;*
> *persecuted, but not abandoned;*
> *struck down, but not destroyed.*

Therefore we do not lose heart.
Though outwardly we are wasting away,
> yet inwardly we are being renewed day by day.

My afflictions are momentary and
> don't compare to the glory

that will unveil a testimony, a story,
a song I will sing all day long praising our Savior
Who delivered me from another one.

About the Author

Rian N. Jenkins has been in love with writing since sixth grade. Close to thirty years, she has inspired, entertained, and educated many through poetry, novellas, journalism, and performances. After becoming a published author in 2021, this book is her third poetry anthology. Along with being a gifted writer, she has been a middle school teacher for nineteen years.

She is the mother of Joshua. In her spare time, she loves to watch sports—especially football—thrift, and read a lot of YA lit she shares with her students and the world via YouTube.

Check out her website, WWW.RIANNJENKINS.COM

www.ingramcontent.com/pod-product-compliance
Lightning Source LLC
Chambersburg PA
CBHW072221070526
44585CB00015B/1441